The Definitive Guide to Earning Money on YouTube

Introduction

YouTube has become one of the largest and most popular online platforms in the world. With billions of active users every month, it's no surprise that many people are exploring ways to earn money through this channel. Whether you're a content creator, marketer, or just looking to supplement your income, YouTube can be an incredibly lucrative platform if used correctly.

However, monetizing a YouTube channel is not as straightforward as simply uploading videos. There are many factors to consider, from the type of content you produce to the way you market yourself and your channel. The advertising and sponsorship landscape can be complex and confusing, and without the right strategy and approach, it can be difficult to make a significant income from YouTube.

This eBook, "The Definitive Guide to Earning Money on YouTube," is designed to help you navigate this landscape and unlock the full potential of your channel. In these pages, you will learn everything you need to know about monetizing your YouTube channel, including:

The different ways to make money on YouTube, from advertising and sponsorships to merchandise sales and crowdfunding.
How to grow your audience and build a brand that appeals to advertisers and sponsors.
The technical and legal requirements for monetizing your channel, and how to get started with Google AdSense.
Best practices for creating and promoting high-quality content that engages your audience and drives revenue.

The most effective marketing and promotional strategies for building a sustainable, profitable channel.
Whether you're just starting out or looking to take your YouTube income to the next level, "The Definitive Guide to Earning Money on YouTube" provides the knowledge, insights, and tools you need to succeed. So why wait? Start your journey to YouTube success today!

Index

1. AdSense Revenue Sharing
2. Sponsored Content and Product Placements
3. Affiliate Marketing
4. Digital Products and Services Sales
5. Merchandise Sales
6. Crowdfunding
7. Subscriptions and Memberships
8. Online Courses and Workshops
9. Live Streaming and Virtual Events
10. Donations and Tips
11. Licensing and Repurposing Content
12. Brand Deals and Collaborations
13. Consulting and Coaching Services
14. Public Speaking and Workshops
15. Writing and Self-Publishing Books
16. Building and Selling Online Tools
17. Network and Affiliate Programs
18. Selling Physical Products
19. Virtual Summits and Conferences
20. Sponsored Social Media Posts and Influencer Marketing

Chapter 1
AdSense Revenue Sharing

AdSense is a program run by Google that allows website owners and YouTube content creators to make money by displaying ads on their platforms. The program operates on a revenue-sharing model, where advertisers pay Google for ad space on participating websites and videos, and a portion of the revenue is then passed on to the content creators.

To participate in AdSense, you must first apply and be approved by Google. You'll then need to add the AdSense code to your website or enable monetization on your YouTube channel. Once set up, you can start earning money from ads displayed on your platform. The amount you earn will depend on several factors, including the type of ad, the location of your audience, and the size of your platform.

One way to increase your AdSense earnings is by optimizing your platform for ad display. This includes choosing the right ad format and placement, as well as making sure your content is appropriate for advertising. You can also choose to display ads from specific advertisers, or opt to display only certain types of ads.

Another way to maximize your AdSense earnings is by growing your audience. The more people who visit your website or watch your videos, the more opportunities you'll have to display ads and earn money. This can be accomplished through various strategies, such as creating high-quality content, promoting your platform through social media, and optimizing your website for search engines.

It's also important to be aware of the AdSense program policies and guidelines. This includes ad placement rules, content restrictions, and guidelines for click fraud and invalid traffic. Violating these policies can result in your account being suspended or terminated, so it's important to familiarize yourself with them and follow them closely.

In conclusion, AdSense is a great way for website owners and YouTube content creators to monetize their platforms and earn money from ad revenue. By optimizing your platform and growing your audience, you can maximize your AdSense earnings and enjoy a steady stream of income from your online presence. As long as you follow the program's policies and guidelines, AdSense can be a valuable tool for earning money through your website or YouTube channel

Chapter 2
Sponsored Content and Product Placements

Sponsored content and product placements on YouTube is a way for content creators to earn money by promoting products and services through their videos. This can be done through paid sponsorships, brand deals, or product placements, where the content creator mentions or demonstrates the use of a product or service.

In a sponsored content deal, the content creator is paid by a brand or advertiser to create a video that promotes their product or service. This can be done in the form of a product review, tutorial, or other type of video that showcases the product or service in a positive light.

Product placements, on the other hand, involve the content creator mentioning or demonstrating the use of a product or service in a video, without the video being specifically created for the product. This type of placement can be more subtle and less overt than a sponsored content deal, but can still be an effective way to promote a product or service.

Sponsored content and product placements provide content creators with a way to earn money by promoting products and services to their audience. They also allow brands and advertisers to reach a larger audience and promote their products and services in a more engaging and entertaining way.

To start with sponsored content and product placements on YouTube, content creators must have a large and engaged audience, as well as a good reputation and brand image. They will also need to be proactive in reaching out to brands and advertisers and negotiating deals.

Once a deal is in place, content creators can start creating and uploading videos that promote the product or service. They must also disclose that the video is sponsored or that the product is a paid placement, in accordance with advertising regulations and YouTube's guidelines.

To effectively promote products and services through sponsored content and product placements, content creators can use a variety of tactics, including showcasing the product in a positive light, demonstrating its use and benefits, and engaging with their audience through comments and discussion. Additionally, they can use social media and other marketing channels to drive traffic to their YouTube channel and promote their sponsored content and product placements.

In conclusion, sponsored content and product placements on YouTube provide content creators with a way to earn money by promoting products and services through their videos. To get started, content creators need a large and engaged audience, as well as a good reputation and brand image. By effectively promoting products and services through sponsored content and product placements, they can earn money, build their brand, and reach a larger audience

Chapter 3

Affiliate Marketing

Affiliate marketing on YouTube is a way for content creators to earn money by promoting other people's products and services and earning a commission for each sale or lead generated through their affiliate link.

To participate in affiliate marketing on YouTube, content creators must first join an affiliate program, such as Amazon Associates or Commission Junction. They will then be given a unique affiliate link to promote the products and services of the affiliate program.

When a viewer clicks on the affiliate link in a video description or annotation, they are redirected to the product or service page where they can complete a purchase. If a sale is made or a lead is generated, the content creator earns a commission, typically a percentage of the sale price.

Affiliate marketing on YouTube provides content creators with a way to monetize their channel and earn money by promoting products and services that align with their content. It also allows them to reach a larger audience by promoting products and services that their viewers may be interested in.

To start with affiliate marketing on YouTube, content creators must first join an affiliate program and obtain a unique affiliate link. They must also have a YouTube channel in good standing and meet the requirements set by the affiliate program.

Once they have the affiliate link, content creators can start promoting products and services in their videos. This can include product reviews, unboxing videos, or tutorials that demonstrate the use of a product. When promoting the products, content creators must ensure that they disclose that they are using an affiliate link and that they will earn a commission for any sales generated through the link.

To effectively promote affiliate products and services, content creators can use a variety of tactics, including mentioning the products in their videos, including links in the video description, and creating dedicated promotional videos. Additionally, they can use social media and other marketing channels to drive traffic to their YouTube channel and promote their affiliate products and services.

In conclusion, affiliate marketing on YouTube is a way for content creators to monetize their channel and earn money by promoting products and services from an affiliate program. To get started, content creators need to join an affiliate program, obtain a unique affiliate link, and have a YouTube channel in good standing. By promoting affiliate products and services effectively, they can drive sales, earn commissions, and grow their brand

Chapter 4
Digital Products and Services Sales

Digital products and services sales on YouTube is a way for content creators to monetize their channel by selling digital products and services related to their brand or content. This can include ebooks, courses, webinars, consulting services, and more.

YouTube provides content creators with several tools to sell their digital products and services directly from their channel. For example, they can use the YouTube Creator Studio to create and publish links to their products, which can appear in the video description or as annotations in the video.

When a viewer clicks on a link to a digital product or service, they are redirected to the creator's website or landing page where they can complete the purchase. The payment processing and transaction handling is handled by the creator's payment processor.

Selling digital products and services on YouTube provides content creators with an additional source of income and a way to monetize their channel. It also allows them to reach a larger audience by offering their expertise and knowledge through digital products and services.

To start selling digital products and services on YouTube, content creators must have a website or landing page where they can sell their products and handle transactions. They will also need a payment processor, such as PayPal or Stripe, to process payments and handle transactions.

Once the website or landing page is set up, content creators can start creating and uploading their digital products and services. This can include ebooks, courses, webinars, consulting services, and more. They will need to provide information about their products, including descriptions, pricing, and any promotional materials.

To promote their digital products and services, content creators can use several tactics, including mentioning their products in their videos, including links in the video description, and creating dedicated promotional videos. Additionally, they can use social media and other marketing channels to drive traffic to their YouTube channel and promote their products.

In conclusion, selling digital products and services on YouTube provides content creators with an additional source of income and a way to monetize their channel. By offering digital products and services related to their brand or content, they are able to reach a larger audience and provide value to their viewers. To get started, content creators need a website or landing page, a payment processor, and the ability to create and upload their digital products and services. By promoting their products effectively, they can drive sales and grow their brand

Chapter 5
Merchandise Sales

Merchandise sales on YouTube are a way for content creators to earn money from their channel by selling products related to their brand or content. The products can range from t-shirts, hoodies, mugs, stickers, and other merchandise items that align with their channel theme.

YouTube has a feature called "YouTube Merchandise Shelf" which allows content creators to showcase and sell their merchandise directly from their channel. The shelf appears below the video player and includes product images, descriptions, and pricing information. When a viewer clicks on a product, they are redirected to the seller's website where they can complete the purchase.

YouTube takes a commission of 10-15% on each sale made through the YouTube Merchandise Shelf. The remaining revenue goes directly to the content creator. The commission fee covers the cost of processing payments and handling the transaction.

Selling merchandise on YouTube is an effective way for content creators to monetize their channel and increase their income. It also provides a way for viewers to support their favorite creators by purchasing products that align with their content. By offering merchandise for sale, content creators are able to extend their brand and increase their reach beyond YouTube.

To start selling merchandise on YouTube, content creators must have a YouTube channel that is in good standing and meet certain criteria. They must also have a Google merchant account and connect it to their YouTube channel.

Additionally, creators must have a website where they can sell their products and fulfill orders. The website can be a standalone e-commerce site or an existing platform such as Shopify or BigCommerce.

Once the website and merchant account are set up, content creators can start creating and uploading their products to the YouTube Merchandise Shelf. They will need to provide product information, including images, descriptions, and pricing. When a viewer clicks on a product, they are redirected to the creator's website to complete the purchase.

When it comes to promoting their merchandise, content creators can use a variety of tactics to drive sales. For example, they can include a link to their merchandise in the video description, mention it in their videos, or create dedicated merchandise videos. Additionally, they can use social media to promote their merchandise and drive traffic to their YouTube channel.

In conclusion, merchandise sales on YouTube are a great way for content creators to monetize their channel and increase their income. By offering merchandise related to their brand or content, they are able to extend their reach beyond YouTube and provide a way for viewers to support their favorite creators. To get started, content creators need to have a YouTube channel in good standing, a website, and a Google merchant account. By promoting their merchandise effectively, they can drive sales and grow their brand

Chapter 6
Crowdfunding

Crowdfunding is a way for creators to raise funds from their audience to support their projects. On YouTube, creators can use crowdfunding to finance their content production or other expenses related to their channel. There are several crowdfunding platforms that creators can use to set up a campaign, such as Patreon, Kickstarter, and Indiegogo.

Patreon is a platform that allows creators to earn a recurring income from their fans. Fans can support creators by making a monthly pledge, and in return, they get access to exclusive perks and benefits, such as early access to videos, behind-the-scenes content, and more. Patreon takes a percentage of the creator's earnings, and the rest is sent to the creator.

Kickstarter is a platform that allows creators to raise funds for a specific project. Creators set a funding goal and deadline, and if they reach their goal, they get to keep the funds raised. Kickstarter operates on an all-or-nothing model, meaning that if the goal is not reached, the creators don't receive any funding. Kickstarter takes a percentage of the funds raised, and the rest is sent to the creators.

Indiegogo is a platform that allows creators to raise funds for their projects, similar to Kickstarter. Creators can set a funding goal and deadline, and if they reach their goal, they get to keep the funds raised. Indiegogo operates on a flexible funding model, meaning that creators keep the funds raised, even if they don't reach their goal. Indiegogo takes a percentage of the funds raised, and the rest is sent to the creators.

Crowdfunding can be a great way for creators to finance their projects and get support from their fans. However, it's important for creators to keep in mind that crowdfunding is not a guarantee of funding. They need to have a clear plan, engage with their audience, and offer compelling perks and benefits to encourage people to support their projects.

In addition to crowdfunding, YouTube also offers other monetization options, such as subscriptions and memberships, ads, YouTube Premium revenue sharing, Super Chat, and channel memberships. By using these monetization options, creators can diversify their income streams and make money while creating and sharing the content they love.

In conclusion, crowdfunding is a way for creators to raise funds from their audience to support their projects. There are several crowdfunding platforms available, such as Patreon, Kickstarter, and Indiegogo, which creators can use to set up a campaign. Crowdfunding can be a great way for creators to finance their projects, but it's important for them to have a clear plan, engage with their audience, and offer compelling perks and benefits. In addition to crowdfunding, YouTube offers several other monetization options, such as subscriptions and memberships, ads, YouTube Premium revenue sharing, Super Chat, and channel memberships

Chapter 7
Subscriptions and Memberships

YouTube Subscriptions and Memberships allow content creators to earn money by offering exclusive benefits to their subscribers. In order to start making money through subscriptions and memberships, a content creator must have a verified YouTube channel with over 1,000 subscribers.

Subscriptions are a way for viewers to support their favorite creators on a recurring basis by paying a monthly fee. In return, subscribers get access to exclusive content, perks, and a special badge indicating their support. Creators earn a portion of the subscription fee, typically 55%.

YouTube Memberships are a new way for creators to monetize their content and engage with their audience. With memberships, creators can offer exclusive perks and benefits to their viewers, including custom emoji, exclusive live streams, early access to videos, and more. Creators can set the membership fee and earn a portion of it, typically 70%.

To start a membership, a content creator must have a minimum of 100 subscribers. They can then go to the "Memberships" section in the YouTube Studio and set up the membership. They can choose the perks they want to offer, set the price, and customize the membership page.

In addition to subscriptions and memberships, YouTube also offers other ways for creators to monetize their content, such as ads, YouTube Premium revenue sharing, Super Chat, and channel memberships.

Ads are the most traditional way of making money on YouTube. Creators earn money when viewers watch ads that are placed before, during, or after their videos. The revenue is split between YouTube and the creator, with the creator typically earning 55% of the ad revenue.

YouTube Premium revenue sharing is a program that allows creators to earn a portion of the subscription fee when viewers sign up for YouTube Premium. YouTube Premium is a paid subscription service that offers ad-free viewing, access to exclusive content, and offline video playback.

Super Chat is a feature that allows viewers to pay to highlight their comments during live streams. Creators earn a portion of the Super Chat revenue, typically 70%.

Channel Memberships are a way for viewers to support their favorite creators by paying a monthly fee. In return, they get access to exclusive perks and benefits, such as custom badges, special emoji, and members-only live streams. Creators earn a portion of the channel membership fee, typically 70%.

In conclusion, YouTube Subscriptions and Memberships provide a new way for content creators to monetize their content and engage with their audience. Creators can offer exclusive perks and benefits to their subscribers, and earn money from the subscription fee. In addition to subscriptions and memberships, YouTube also offers other monetization options, such as ads, YouTube Premium revenue sharing, Super Chat, and channel memberships. By using these monetization options, content creators can make money while creating and sharing the content they love

Chapter 8
Online Courses and Workshops

Online courses and workshops are becoming an increasingly popular way for creators to monetize their content on YouTube. Here's a complete summary of how they can do so:

Online Courses:

Online courses are pre-recorded or live-streamed educational content that can be accessed by students at any time.
Creators can monetize their courses through various methods, including selling access to the course, offering a subscription model, or charging for individual lessons.
To get started with offering online courses on YouTube, creators must have a solid understanding of their subject matter and be able to deliver high-quality content.
They can use YouTube as a platform to promote their courses and provide a sneak peek of the content, but may need to use a third-party tool to deliver the actual course materials.
Workshops:

Workshops are live-streamed or pre-recorded events that provide hands-on instruction and interactive activities for attendees.

Creators can monetize their workshops by selling tickets, offering a subscription model, or charging for individual sessions.

To get started with hosting workshops on YouTube, creators must have a solid understanding of their subject matter and be able to deliver engaging and interactive content.

They can use YouTube's built-in live streaming feature or a third-party tool to broadcast their workshops and interact with attendees in real-time.

In conclusion, offering online courses and workshops can provide creators with additional monetization opportunities on YouTube. By delivering high-quality educational content and engaging with their audience, creators can build a following and generate revenue. It's important for creators to ensure that their courses and workshops are in line with YouTube's policies and guidelines and provide a safe and enjoyable experience for their students.

Chapter 9
Live Streaming and Virtual Events

YouTube provides creators with the ability to make money through live streaming and virtual events. Here's a complete summary of how they can do so:

Live Streaming:

Live streaming allows creators to interact with their audience in real-time and provides a unique viewing experience. Creators can monetize their live streams through various methods, including Super Chat, which allows viewers to pay to have their message highlighted in the chat and seen by

the creator, Channel Memberships, which allows viewers to pay a monthly fee for access to exclusive content and perks, and advertisements, which play during the live stream and generate revenue for the creator.
To get started with live streaming on YouTube, creators must have a verified account, an active YouTube channel, and an up-to-date encoder.
They can then use YouTube's built-in live streaming feature or a third-party tool to broadcast their content.
Virtual Events:

Virtual events are live-streamed or pre-recorded events that take place online instead of in-person.
They provide a way for creators to connect with their audience and monetize their content while adhering to social distancing guidelines.
Creators can monetize virtual events through various methods, including ticket sales, sponsorships, and advertisements.
To get started with hosting virtual events on YouTube, creators must have a verified account, an active YouTube channel, and an up-to-date encoder.
They can then use YouTube's built-in live streaming feature or a third-party tool to broadcast their event.
In conclusion, live streaming and virtual events provide creators with additional monetization opportunities on YouTube. By engaging with their audience and delivering high-quality content, creators can generate revenue and grow their following. It's important for creators to be mindful of YouTube's policies and guidelines and to ensure that their live streams and virtual events provide a safe and enjoyable experience for their audience

Chapter 10
Donations and Tips

YouTube is a platform where creators can upload videos and earn money through various monetization methods such as advertisements, sponsorships, memberships, and donations. Here's a complete summary of the ways in which creators can make money through donations and tips on YouTube:

Donations:

Donations are financial contributions made by viewers directly to the creator's channel.
YouTube doesn't take a cut from the donations received, but the payment processing fees may apply.
Creators can receive donations through third-party services like Patreon, Ko-fi, or PayPal.
Viewers can make donations by clicking on a link provided by the creator in the video description or through the chat during a live stream.
Tips:

Tips are similar to donations but are often smaller in amount and made in response to a specific request from the creator.
YouTube has integrated the feature of tipping into its platform and partnered with third-party providers like PayPal.
Tips can be sent through Super Chat during a live stream, which is a paid feature that allows viewers to highlight their messages in the chat and stand out to the creator.
YouTube also has a feature called Channel Memberships, which allows viewers to pay a monthly fee to access exclusive content and perks provided by the creator.
To get started with monetizing through donations and tips on YouTube, creators must first enable monetization on their channel and comply with YouTube's policies and guidelines. They also need to have a linked AdSense account to receive payments.

In conclusion, while donations and tips are not the main source of income for most creators on YouTube, they can provide a supplementary stream of revenue. By providing engaging and valuable content, creators can build a dedicated community of fans who are willing to support them financially through these monetization methods

Chapter 11
Licensing and Repurposing Content

Licensing and Repurposing Content in YouTube is a way for content creators to monetize their videos by licensing their content to other parties. This can involve granting permission for other parties to use their videos for various purposes, such as commercials, film, or TV shows.

In licensing arrangements, content creators may charge a fee for the use of their videos, or they may receive a percentage of the profits from the commercial use of their content. This type of arrangement is especially beneficial for content creators who have created high-quality, engaging videos that have the potential to be repurposed for other purposes.

Repurposing content involves reusing existing videos for different purposes. For example, a content creator may create a video for their YouTube channel, and then license it to a brand for use in a commercial. This type of arrangement allows content creators to maximize the value of their videos, as they can be reused multiple times, generating income each time.

One of the benefits of licensing and repurposing content is the ability to earn a passive income. Content creators can license their videos once and receive ongoing payments, without having to put in additional effort. This can be a great way to monetize their channel and increase their income.

Another advantage is the exposure that licensing and repurposing can bring. When content creators license their videos, they are potentially exposing their work to a wider audience, increasing their visibility and potentially leading to new opportunities.

However, it's important to be aware of the legal implications of licensing and repurposing content. Content creators should ensure that they have the necessary permissions to license their videos and that they are in compliance with copyright laws. It's also important to have a clear agreement in place with the licensing party, specifying the terms of the arrangement and protecting the content creator's rights.

In conclusion, licensing and repurposing content in YouTube can be a lucrative way for content creators to monetize their channel and increase their income. By licensing their videos and maximizing the value of their content, content creators can earn a passive income and gain exposure to a wider audience. However, it's important to be aware of the legal implications and to ensure that the licensing arrangement is clear and fair

Chapter 12
Brand Deals and Collaborations

Brand Deals and Collaborations in YouTube are a form of monetization for YouTubers and other content creators. In these arrangements, content creators partner with brands to create sponsored content that promotes the brand's products or services. This can take many forms, including product placement, sponsored videos, and affiliate marketing.

Product placement involves the integration of a brand's products into a content creator's regular videos, usually through demonstrations, reviews, or casual mentions. This type of arrangement can be a natural and unobtrusive way for brands to promote their products, as the content creator's followers are likely to trust their recommendations.

Sponsored videos are similar, but they are more focused on promoting a brand's products or services. In these videos, the content creator creates a video specifically to promote a brand's product, often in exchange for payment or a free product. The video may include a review, demonstration, or endorsement of the product.

Affiliate marketing involves the content creator promoting a brand's products or services through a unique affiliate link. When a viewer clicks the link and makes a purchase, the content creator earns a commission. This type of arrangement is often used by content creators who want to monetize their channel without having to create sponsored content.

One of the key benefits of brand deals and collaborations for content creators is the ability to earn a steady stream of income from their channel. By partnering with brands, content creators can supplement their advertising revenue and potentially increase their earnings.

For brands, these partnerships offer a way to reach a wider audience and increase brand awareness. By partnering with content creators, brands can tap into the trust that the content creator's followers have in them and the recommendations they make.

However, it's essential to choose the right brand to partner with and to ensure that the sponsored content is clearly marked as such. Content creators should also be careful not to compromise their credibility by promoting products or services that they do not believe in or that do not align with their values.

In conclusion, brand deals and collaborations in YouTube can be a win-win for both content creators and brands. By partnering with the right brands and creating engaging, high-quality sponsored content, content creators can monetize their channel and increase their income. At the same time, brands can reach a wider audience and increase brand awareness, leading to increased sales and a more loyal customer base

Chapter 13
Consulting and Coaching Services

Consulting and coaching services on YouTube can be a source of income for content creators who have expertise and knowledge in a specific field. These services may include offering personal and professional development advice, offering business and marketing strategies, or providing technical support and tutorials.

One way for YouTube content creators to make money through consulting and coaching services is by offering paid consultations or coaching sessions. This can be done through video calls, live streams, or other methods. The content creator can set their own rates and schedule sessions with clients who are interested in their services.

Another way to make money through consulting and coaching services on YouTube is by offering online courses or coaching programs. These programs may be sold through the content creator's website or through online platforms like Udemy. The content creator can leverage their expertise and experience to create a comprehensive course or program that teaches others how to achieve specific goals.

In addition, content creators can make money through consulting and coaching services by monetizing their

YouTube channel. This can be done by integrating affiliate marketing, sponsored content, and product placements into their videos. By promoting products and services that are relevant to their audience and expertise, content creators can earn a commission for every sale generated through their videos.

It's important to note that to be successful in offering consulting and coaching services on YouTube, content creators must have a strong understanding of their target audience and their needs. They must also be knowledgeable and credible in their area of expertise, and able to effectively communicate their ideas and strategies.

Furthermore, it's important for content creators to have a clear and consistent message and brand identity. This can help them build trust with their audience and establish themselves as experts in their field.

In conclusion, consulting and coaching services on YouTube can be a lucrative source of income for content creators who have expertise and knowledge in a specific field. To make money through these services, content creators can offer paid consultations, create online courses, monetize their YouTube channel, and more. By understanding their target audience, having a strong brand identity, and effectively communicating their ideas and strategies, content creators can build a successful business and make money through consulting and coaching services on YouTube.

Chapter 14
Public Speaking and Workshops

Public speaking and workshops can be a source of income for YouTube content creators who have expertise and knowledge in a specific field. These services provide a platform for content creators to share their ideas and strategies with a larger audience, and can be an effective way to make money through their YouTube channel.

One way for content creators to make money through public speaking and workshops is by offering paid events and workshops. This can include in-person or virtual speaking engagements, as well as online workshops and webinars. The content creator can set their own rates and schedule events with organizations or individuals who are interested in their services.

Another way to make money through public speaking and workshops on YouTube is by offering courses and training programs. This can include online courses and workshops that teach others how to achieve specific goals or develop specific skills. The content creator can leverage their expertise and experience to create comprehensive programs that are valuable and relevant to their audience.

In addition, content creators can monetize their YouTube channel by integrating affiliate marketing, sponsored content, and product placements into their public speaking and workshop videos. By promoting products and services that are relevant to their audience and expertise, content creators can earn a commission for every sale generated through their videos.

It's important for content creators to have a clear and engaging speaking style, as well as a strong understanding of their audience and their needs. They must also be knowledgeable and credible in their area of expertise, and able to effectively communicate their ideas and strategies.

Furthermore, it's important for content creators to have a clear and consistent message and brand identity. This can help them build trust with their audience and establish themselves as experts in their field.

In conclusion, public speaking and workshops can be a lucrative source of income for YouTube content creators who have expertise and knowledge in a specific field. To make money through these services, content creators can offer paid events and workshops, create online courses and training programs, monetize their YouTube channel, and more. By having a clear and engaging speaking style, understanding their audience, and having a strong brand identity, content creators can build a successful business and make money through public speaking and workshops on YouTube

Chapter 15
Writing and Self-Publishing Books

Writing and self-publishing books can be a profitable venture, especially with the growth of online platforms such as YouTube. Here is a complete summary of how you can make money writing and self-publishing books through YouTube:

Write your book: Start by deciding on the topic you want to write about. You can write fiction or non-fiction, depending on your interests and strengths. Be sure to research your subject thoroughly and create a detailed outline before you start writing.

Edit and proofread: Once you have finished writing, it is important to edit and proofread your book. This will help you eliminate any errors and ensure that your book is of high quality. You can hire an editor or use online tools such as Grammarly to help you.

Format your book: Once your book is ready, you need to format it for self-publishing. You can use tools such as

Kindle Direct Publishing (KDP) to format your book for Kindle or CreateSpace to format your book for print.

Publish your book: You can self-publish your book on platforms such as Amazon Kindle Direct Publishing (KDP), which will make your book available for sale on Amazon. You can also publish your book in print format on platforms such as CreateSpace.

Promote your book: Once your book is published, you need to promote it to reach your target audience. You can use social media platforms such as Facebook, Twitter, and Instagram to promote your book. You can also use YouTube to promote your book by creating videos that showcase your book and by providing book reviews.

Monetize your YouTube channel: You can monetize your YouTube channel by allowing ads to be displayed on your videos. You will earn money from these ads based on the number of views your videos receive. Additionally, you can sell your book on your YouTube channel, providing links to your book's sales page on Amazon.

Collaborate with other YouTubers: You can also collaborate with other YouTubers who have a similar target audience to yours. You can guest post on their channels, or they can guest post on yours. This will help you reach a wider audience and potentially increase sales of your book.

In conclusion, writing and self-publishing books through YouTube can be a profitable venture. You need to write a high-quality book, publish it on platforms such as Amazon KDP, promote it on YouTube and other social media platforms, monetize your YouTube channel, and collaborate with other YouTubers. With dedication and hard work, you can make money from your writing and self-publishing efforts.

Chapter 16

Building and Selling Online Tools

Building and selling online tools through YouTube can be a lucrative business. Here is a complete summary of how you can make money by building and selling online tools through YouTube:

Identify a need: The first step in building and selling online tools is to identify a need in the market. This can be done by researching the needs of your target audience, such as small business owners or marketers, and identifying gaps in the current offerings.

Build the tool: Once you have identified a need, you can start building your online tool. This can involve using existing technology or programming languages, or developing your own custom solution.

Test and refine the tool: Once the tool is built, you need to test it thoroughly to ensure it meets the needs of your target audience. This can involve getting feedback from beta users, and making any necessary adjustments to improve the tool.

Create a sales page: Once your online tool is ready to be sold, you need to create a sales page. This should include a detailed description of the tool, its features and benefits, and a clear call-to-action. You can also include testimonials from beta users to build credibility.

Promote the tool on YouTube: You can use YouTube to promote your online tool to reach your target audience. You can create videos that showcase the tool and demonstrate how it can be used, or provide a review of the tool. You can also create tutorials and how-to guides to help users get the most out of the tool.

Monetize your YouTube channel: You can monetize your YouTube channel by allowing ads to be displayed on your videos. You will earn money from these ads based on the number of views your videos receive. Additionally, you can sell your online tool on your YouTube channel, providing links to your sales page.

Collaborate with other YouTubers: You can also collaborate with other YouTubers who have a similar target audience to yours. You can guest post on their channels, or they can guest post on yours. This will help you reach a wider audience and potentially increase sales of your tool.

In conclusion, building and selling online tools through YouTube can be a profitable business. You need to identify a need in the market, build a high-quality tool, create a sales page, promote the tool on YouTube and other social media platforms, monetize your YouTube channel, and collaborate with other YouTubers. With dedication and hard work, you can make money from your online tool business

Chapter 17
Network and Affiliate Programs

Using network and affiliate programs on YouTube can be a great way to earn money. Here is a complete summary of how you can make money through network and affiliate programs on YouTube:

Choose the right network: There are many affiliate networks available, so it's important to choose one that is right for your niche. Consider factors such as the commission structure, product selection, and support offered by the network. Some popular affiliate networks for YouTubers include Amazon Associates, Commission Junction, and Clickbank.

Choose the right products: Once you have joined a network, you need to choose the products you want to promote. Choose products that are relevant to your niche and that you believe in. Be sure to research each product thoroughly and test it out before promoting it to your audience.

Create content: You need to create content that showcases the products you are promoting. This can be in the form of product reviews, tutorials, or demonstrations. Your content should be engaging and provide valuable information to your audience.

Add affiliate links: Once your content is ready, you need to add your affiliate links to it. These links will track clicks and sales, and you will earn a commission for each sale that is made through your links. Be sure to follow the guidelines of your affiliate network and disclose that you are using affiliate links in your content.

Promote your content: You need to promote your content to reach your target audience. You can use social media platforms such as Facebook, Twitter, and Instagram to promote your content. You can also use YouTube to promote your content by creating videos that showcase your products and by providing product reviews.

Monetize your YouTube channel: You can monetize your YouTube channel by allowing ads to be displayed on your videos. You will earn money from these ads based on the number of views your videos receive. Additionally, you can use your YouTube channel to promote your affiliate products, providing links to your affiliate links in your videos and in the description of your videos.

Collaborate with other YouTubers: You can also collaborate with other YouTubers who have a similar target audience to yours. You can guest post on their channels, or they can guest post on yours. This will help you reach a wider audience and potentially increase sales of your affiliate products.

In conclusion, using network and affiliate programs on YouTube can be a profitable venture. You need to choose the right network and products, create engaging content, add affiliate links, promote your content, monetize your YouTube channel, and collaborate with other YouTubers. With dedication and hard work, you can make money from your network and affiliate program efforts

Chapter 18
Selling Physical Products

Selling physical products through YouTube can be a profitable business venture. Here is a complete summary of how you can make money by selling physical products through YouTube:

Choose the right products: The first step is to choose the right products to sell. Consider factors such as demand, competition, profit margins, and shipping costs. You can sell products that you have created yourself or products that you source from wholesalers.

Create content: You need to create content that showcases your products. This can be in the form of product demonstrations, tutorials, or reviews. Your content should be engaging and provide valuable information to your audience.

Set up a website: You need to set up a website where you can sell your products. You can use platforms such as Shopify or WooCommerce to create your website. Make sure your website is easy to navigate and provides all the information your customers need to make a purchase.

Promote your products: You need to promote your products to reach your target audience. You can use social media platforms such as Facebook, Twitter, and Instagram to promote your products. You can also use YouTube to promote your products by creating videos that showcase your products and by providing product reviews.

Monetize your YouTube channel: You can monetize your YouTube channel by allowing ads to be displayed on your videos. You will earn money from these ads based on the number of views your videos receive. Additionally, you can use your YouTube channel to promote your products, providing links to your website in your videos and in the description of your videos.

Collaborate with other YouTubers: You can also collaborate with other YouTubers who have a similar target audience to yours. You can guest post on their channels, or they can guest post on yours. This will help you reach a wider audience and potentially increase sales of your products.

Fulfill orders: Once an order is placed, you need to fulfill it. This involves packaging and shipping the product to the customer. You can use a fulfillment service such as Fulfillment by Amazon (FBA) to handle the fulfillment process for you.

In conclusion, selling physical products through YouTube can be a profitable venture. You need to choose the right products, create engaging content, set up a website, promote your products, monetize your YouTube channel, collaborate with other YouTubers, and fulfill orders. With dedication and hard work, you can make money from selling physical products through YouTube

Chapter 19
Virtual Summits and Conferences

Hosting virtual summits and conferences on YouTube can be a great way to earn money. Here is a complete summary of how you can make money by hosting virtual summits and conferences on YouTube:

Choose a niche: The first step is to choose a niche for your virtual summit or conference. Consider a topic that you are passionate about and that has a large and engaged audience. You can choose a niche related to your existing YouTube channel or a new niche that you are interested in exploring.

Identify speakers: You need to identify and invite speakers for your virtual summit or conference. Choose speakers who are experts in your chosen niche and who have a large and engaged following. You can offer speakers compensation, such as a percentage of ticket sales, or you can offer them exposure in exchange for speaking at your event.

Set a date and time: Choose a date and time for your virtual summit or conference that is convenient for your speakers and your target audience. Make sure to allow enough time for planning and promoting your event.

Promote your event: You need to promote your event to reach your target audience. You can use social media platforms such as Facebook, Twitter, and Instagram to promote your event. You can also use YouTube to promote your event by creating videos that showcase your event and by providing updates on the speakers and sessions.

Sell tickets: You need to sell tickets for your virtual summit or conference. You can sell tickets through your website or through a platform such as Eventbrite. You can charge a fee for attendance or you can offer the event for free and earn money through sponsorships or advertising.

Host the event: You need to host the event on YouTube. You can use YouTube Live to stream your event and interact with your audience. You can also use tools such as

Zoom or Google Meet to conduct panel discussions or Q&A sessions.

Monetize your YouTube channel: You can monetize your YouTube channel by allowing ads to be displayed on your videos. You will earn money from these ads based on the number of views your videos receive. Additionally, you can use your YouTube channel to promote your event, providing links to your ticket sales page in your videos and in the description of your videos.

In conclusion, hosting virtual summits and conferences on YouTube can be a profitable venture. You need to choose a niche, identify speakers, set a date and time, promote your event, sell tickets, host the event, and monetize your YouTube channel. With dedication and hard work, you can make money from your virtual summit or conference efforts

Chapter 20
Sponsored Social Media Posts and Influencer Marketing

Sponsored Social Media Posts and Influencer Marketing in YouTube are popular methods for companies to promote their products and services, reach a wider audience, and increase sales. Both approaches involve partnering with influencers who have a large following on social media platforms like YouTube, Instagram, or Twitter.

In Sponsored Social Media Posts, companies pay influencers to promote their products or services by posting about them on their social media accounts. These posts can be in the form of photos, videos, or written content, and usually include a call to action, such as "click the link to buy now." This type of promotion is highly effective because it taps into the trust that influencer's followers have in them and the recommendations they make.

Influencer Marketing in YouTube is similar, but the focus is on video content. Companies pay influencers to create sponsored videos promoting their products or services, which can be integrated into the influencer's regular content or be a standalone video. This approach allows companies to reach a more engaged audience, as video content tends to be more captivating and interactive than other forms of social media posts.

One of the key advantages of both Sponsored Social Media Posts and Influencer Marketing in YouTube is the ability to reach a target audience. By partnering with influencers in a specific niche, companies can reach people who are likely to be interested in their products or services, making it easier to convert them into customers.

Another benefit is increased brand awareness. When influencers promote a product or service, their followers are exposed to it, and may become aware of the brand for the first time. This increased visibility can lead to increased sales and a more loyal customer base.

However, it's important to choose the right influencer to partner with. The influencer should have a large, engaged following that is relevant to the target audience, and their content should align with the brand's values and message. It's also essential to have clear, measurable goals in place before entering into a partnership, so that the success of the campaign can be evaluated.

Finally, it's important to ensure that the sponsored content is clearly marked as such, in accordance with advertising regulations. This can be done by including a disclaimer such as "sponsored" or "ad."

In conclusion, Sponsored Social Media Posts and Influencer Marketing in YouTube can be a highly effective way for companies to promote their products and services, reach a wider audience, and increase sales. By choosing the right influencer and having clear, measurable goals in place, companies can see great results from these marketing strategies

www.ingramcontent.com/pod-product-compliance
Lightning Source LLC
Chambersburg PA
CBHW070321220526
45465CB00013B/2115